Aether

Lamine Pearlheart

OTHER BOOKS BY THE SAME AUTHOR

To Life from the Shadows

The Sunrise Scrolls

The Mayan Twins - At the Edge of Xibalba's Well

PREFACE

I want to start by a disclaimer, lest I be taken seriously, that the title of the book does not indulge in a pretense of sagacity or wisdom from my part, and that the word "Aether" means what it means in the Greek word (αἰθήρ), meaning "upper air" or "pure, fresh air"[1].

When I wrote *the Sunrise Scrolls*, my previous book, I was going through straining times, times that shattered the soul and tested my resolve, times which in a sense took me back and forth to twenty years ago; I found myself engaged in an exercise of processing and reprocessing of everything I have known and held for certain.

As I went through the above process, feebly gasping for pure upper air, I

---

[1] https://en.wikipedia.org/wiki/Aether_(mythology)

realized that I had to reacquaint with myself.

I noticed that like a tree amid a storm I swayed left and right but managed to keep my roots grounded on Earth. I also ricocheted against what I liked and hated in me and decided to choose what made sense.

I learned since that when one is in loss of control, one does not necessarily need to lose consciousness or sense. One may not control the speed of his or her fall into the abyss of extinction, but he or she has the choice of opening one's eyes or closing them; blindness and sight are more often than not a personal choice.

So, opening my eyes, after I shut them down temporarily, I realized that all I had to do was to look back; I saw no fear from where I initially started and I could see the person I was and wanted to be, and though I observe my logical descent into oblivion, like all humans before and after me, I decided not to burden myself with any fear or false hopes going forward.

In a world or changing sentiments, I choose to proceed with reason and not with fear, faith and any arbitrary forms of coercion, threats or terror.

My descent into oblivion started the day it was challenged through my birth and will end, not by my demise, but by the birth of another challenge in that of the continuous birth of the joyful children of today and of tomorrow.

Life in this planet, at least statistically when to it comes to our kind and its sheer will of ingenuity in front of negative odds, continues to tramp death and so I hope would reason.

Table of Contents

To the Sun,

For wherever I went, it was there.

On Life

Let him or her view life ending, he or she that thinks life is to be endured, and they shall see it renewed and understand its intrinsic value.

On Existing

I am the firefly, I don't know my purpose, but to live a day in eternity is a life lived nonetheless

I may not last, but I know I'm here to shine and pass

On and on to begin, re-composed becoming air

My doubts are recurring, but certain I am of the beauty of my fading light

Sooner or later parts of me finding a vine

I am born forever

Fear in absurdity will die

To do good is the secret of my illuminating lines; everything else is but noise in time

See me feeble in the darkness facing the almighty night

My deeds are forever carried by sparks

Like shields by knights, I offer no immunity but protection from the larks

Diamonds in the abyss are diamonds nonetheless

"Between the gods and humankind, I stand and plead for the imperfect kind."

I want to be that kind

I am the firefly and I live today

Anticipation

The heart beats

The eyes in distress search for their mistress

The heart beats

The body shivers in anticipation of her

The soul from its hiding place, cowering behind reasons borrowed from the brain, unbeknownst to the eyes, takes a quick glimpse

There's a scent chasing the air

She is not there but perceived are her lips

The heart beats

The lungs breathe not oxygen, but her scent

The shape of her posture marries the light, a shadow is born and covers the world, but there is no fear, it is her approach made apparent

The heart stops and so does time transparent

A beat remembers the day of its birth and says,
Love

Sanity and wisdom abandon their posts like a startled dove

A tornado hits the sea and sets fire on the water

The impact changes the essence of matter

Shaking his head an eagle, says,

The water is lit,

You shall crave her like freedom a slave

You shall think of her and miss her even when she is there; you will need the surge of the brave

The ears do not want to hear about it

They speak to the echoes of her closing footsteps

The bird in wonder loses a feather

The moon and stars move forward to see better

The waves so far placid, now rage against the rocks

The heart locks

The earth loses its orbit

Andromeda shows up in the horizon

The galaxy blushes

The heart disappears, becomes two into one

The one of two fusing like particles of light in the sun

The one and only motion

The brain refuses to approve the unknown potion

Still, vibrations to arguments mere knife to a gun

Resist can the moon, but to the sun in orbit it shall abide

She stands up; an angel in apparition born of light

He moves, grabs her by the hand, he plants a kiss on her lips

She smiles, laughs as merry as a tulip next to a rose

Of her he just pricked a dose

The sun tries harder to outshine their brilliance, but is now in insignificance

Vain is its grievance

Futile it's attempts

Its system thrown in unbalance, questioned

It's order through love beyond the scope of chaos subdued

The world stops

It's reason like an angry hand pounds

The heart beats
Self-anesthesia

Who am I to judge the horror if everyone of us is a potential of one?

Who am I to seek justification if the world is but endless excuses?

Who am I to be against redemption if we are all bound to fall?

Who dares to say they are always tall?

Pieces of glass laughing at shards

Grazing sheep calling the sun just a star

I have known madness and it has always been mine

I gather the pieces, there's no map to the exit or a guide to reassembling a broken mind

I will grab what I can, a firefly in my hand, I am daring the night with laughter courting the dead

With me to death I carry time as sand in time

What I Observed

The bug never has a problem with the boot; it does not know it exists and when it does it is usually too late

Hope is transcending, madness is not

Light and common sense are allies
Ignorance and fear are not; they are more often than not a sign of the enemy

Pleasant manners are always good investments

Money is not

Enough time is good, plenty of time is the best currency to keep in reserve, better be in readiness wealthy

Empires crumble, yours on yourself is forever eternally recurring

The Echoes in Time

"Who wants to live for ever?" Asked the universe.

"I." Responds the sun.

"We hope that you do." Proclaim all the earthly creatures in unison as they breathe its precious reviving air.

"What is the most precious things you have?" Asked the moon watching the dying late zenith.

"The will to go on." Clamours the fruit fly.

"I offer you the earth and its treasures versus one more day, what is your choice?" Life asked a dead man.

"One day with her by my side." Said he without hesitation.

The sun amazed looks on, "I want to parish like this insignificant man, to know such radiating love makes it all worth enduring even the spite of time. Let them be for I see myself in the consciousness of two becoming one."

Their story lost to us now, but they are but a reflection of us in time.

"With her by my side." Say the echoes in time.

Your Reflection

I watched you in the morning and I watched you at night

You know not where you're going,
not where you've been

I sensed the vibration of your soul

Know the exact colour of your
thoughts

You can come now pretending to be
the owner of your delusions

The source of every sensation you
impart

The right mood is to you unknown

Before you drift again with no
prescription

See the shadows of your aversion
they are painting the heavens

Mind that bridge you are not crossing

Careful be, of the smile you are not giving

It is you the world you are warping

The drums are but the beating of your heart

The sirens you hear, it is you they carry in tomorrow's time

Better find those to whom you relate

Find that connection before it is too late

The air you pollute today is the oxygen you breathe tomorrow

The shit you hand to others, you carried for so long

Who can say that you don't have a piece of it in your mind?

Your full-time job is but paid madness

Trading life precious time for trinkets, racing people you don't know to impress

Now that we had our conversation, guess what I am?

The clock is ticking, I am timing your answers

Counting the attempts,

The drops are at the floodgates, not much containment left

In helping there is no serving

In bravery no remorse

No safety in danger

Fear is no advisor

Council is no politician, and no institutions either

Remember, propaganda was sold before by you it was bought

No product of coercion can last a day if not paid for by the shadows

I leave the answer unanswered

I have made my connection, see you in the sunshine as in the rain

Find me in the reflection, it is you I seek

Beyond the dead and the living there is time

A bit of eternity in disguise

Why Some People Live

I suspect that a lot of people continue to live due to the fear of death rather than the love of life.

On Revolutions

Revolutions are an aberration and never are the true causes of change, they are excuses and never a justification; a subterfuge to hide a precarious evolution through insidious and ruthless forces who would not hesitate tomorrow to send benevolence to the gallows.

On Things Perceived

The starlight preying on the darkness
Courage on fear dumbfounded

Age to time waving goodbyes

The summer to the winter offering a crown
They call it a rainbow

A man poking a piece of wood until it is revealed to be an instrument by sound and him a fiddler

Death, a cruel monster, until the relief from the receding pain is known

Fortune, a blessing, until met is its cruel servants and their fear of loosing it all

Glory, for some a redeeming prize, but nonetheless a fading tide

Love, a great gift, until its object is nowhere to be found

Wisdom, a crude attempt, until the hidden lesson is unveiled

The sunset, the end of the day, until life attempts to pass on to the other side

Birth, a natural phenomenon, until the unintelligible seeds planted yesterday bring joy to the mourning heart

While tears mix in with the smile of the surprised face

Power, an unchallenged dictate, until we meet tyranny swept by old age seeking refuge in senility

Mystification, a secret, until speaks the shallow mind

Fear, a bad investment of your thoughts and precious time

Her, I seek, will I ever be able to find?

When the odds get weighted will I keep calm?

Hunger for her that tamed time and sparked waves of light, will she finally decide?

Will love ever conquer pride?

Will honesty succumb to preying eyes?

Will time find measures to ticking minds?

The sea, I see waving its tides

The earth a hope to the changing ides

Sure, something must remain

Will we ever be able to value time in space?

In the sand of it all, I followed my trail, I saw the hill, I saw the light

Pearls in the night,

They call them stars

Pseudo-truth

In capitalism pseudo-truth is monetized and lies are handed to you freely but with a premium; your ability of discernment.

On Choosing One's Representatives

"You give your car to someone to drive with your kids in it, you better make sure that they know how to drive and drive well."

The Difference

Of pearls and ashes
On roads and highways

On evil's blindness
A resource waster; a hostage to its own stench

Of the Sea and the moon
The sunrise and its temper

The fall and rise; the seasons in tandem
The piano sound giving a turn to the drum

The violin making sense of the stick
The eye, the speed of a blink

The quake vanquished by the deafening height
The secret of the night is but a fading light

A soldier finally seeing the madness of the trench
Time in regression, the floodgates in motion

An infant holding a rock facing a tank
A woman waving a flag of resolution, not budging not even for a marching bone gnawing bank

The condor of the Andes flying higher than the skyscrapers landing on the clouds

"Every state a prison to its citizens before it is an insurmountable border to the desperate immigrants." Says a voice from the clouds

Mortgage rates, death row inmates in common motion
Chains for tomorrow bowing down in pain

Of pearls and ashes
On roads and highways

The speed of light
The vociferous undressed night

The anticipated love
The drumming heart

The one who can and might
The symphony playing at her sight

The uncontrolled progression, the combustion of the self, seeking the same but refined

A defined need, an instinctive drive

The conspiracy of the heart

It wants what it wants; her in broad daylight and at night

If Today Were Your Last Day

"What would you do if you knew that today was your last day?"

I have the answer to that, "You do what you have always done; nothing different."

On the Reason for Living

We have the habit of living so we live.

The Cure

Breaks the sunlight in my confused heart

Shivers the sound in the early morning light

Survival of the fittest is but living and no living at all

Life seeks rhythms and lovers 'call

Pulses, energy, the "I" coming, coming to take you home

Reborn from tragedy seeking no master, ready to roam

Feel the speed of the projection racing

The speed of light too slow for the propulsion

Free from the dying augur, racing the waves and the currents of sunlight

Knowledge of life, no secrets

Moving further and farther

Sun and stars, my beacons to the gates of the universe

Shadows I leave behind to the unwise

Light is my revelation

On Nations

Nations? I don't want to be in someone else's fish tank.

On Charity

Charity is a temporary solution. It is a bridge and you don't live on a bridge, you pass through it.

I see

Through the night, my eyes piercing the veil of time

I see a boy walking his shadows home, his aim is a hill, he is chasing a light

I see a tear through a smile

The uncontrolled urge of being born and not knowing how to forever heal

I see a bulging river afraid of a sea in envy of the placid ocean

I see space, timetables, a firefly in the night

The moon making faces, the earth in motion unseen

Diamonds in the abyss whispering to the stars

I see the idea of her I need, eyes I have seen

Consciousness seeking its pair

Life writing its book in me

I recognize the pattern and now I perceive the aim

I hear the echoes in the depth of clarity

I chased the distraction, fear and noise of the ravenous void

The lightness of benevolence leading the way

All that is must be

All that will be must not wish

All that was cannot

On Happiness

Happiness, a continuous state of bliss, is not of this world, but bursts of joy and contentment leading to an elevated state of gratitude is achievable and can be at hand.

On Presumptions

To think of oneself wise borders on the ignorance

To think of oneself honest is to loudly clamour to the world that you are a thief

To claim the crown of leadership is somewhat to tell the electors of your lack of perception of the weight of responsibility you intend to carry

To say it lightly; watch out for the scoundrel in you for it will lead you on before it does the others

On Fear and Anger

Fear and anger are sometimes unavoidable reactive forces, don't let them lead you to war when you clearly have not yet mastered the regiment of

peace for when peace comes you will be
the only looser.

Who we are

Some of us hang out in low places to
play out the low keys of the piano

Some of us roar like the drums, soon
fading in an ultra tempo

Others are meant to be the soft voice
of the violin
You see them slide undisturbed
beyond the common din

Amongst the echoes of the saxophone
seeking the night are flocks of voices
chanting the daybreak

The sudden flight of the soft flutes
meets the chorus of humankind
charmed by the imperceptible yet
sounding time

The tolling bells shamelessly telling
our short stories in evidence

The confirmation of all that is bound
to die of life

The falling rain covers us as we
disappear

We all meet in insignificance

Fade we will in the beauty of the rose
overpowering the rigidity of the fence

On Cruelty

Adding to what Jacques Brel said
once, "I would rather be a coward than

cruel.", I say, "I would rather look foolish than be cruel."

On the Afterlife

The afterlife? Why do you think that you deserve another life? Have you done a great job with this one?

What it is

I am the particle that thinks
I am the particle that loves
I am the particle that seeks other particles
I am the particle that knows it is but a particle

I am the particle aware of a greater entity itself not a particle

I am the particle that dreams and hopes, for in hoping and dreaming it finds

In the universe of infinite particles, it anticipated and stumbled upon that one important particle that is you

I am the particle of today that will become and will be part of other particles tomorrow

I am the particle that will eventually collide with other particles
In continuous motion it braces itself and others for brushes of imminent curves
It holds no grudges against other particles for it saw and experienced the near end of all particles

It is projected in time that is the present

It knows that the past, as important as it may be, is but a memory

The future is but a construct of the present

The present its only constant

It also knows that the processes are a description of the creation but not the creation itself

That humankind is life aware of itself

Death is vanquished and chased away by every baby particle's birth

The much-touted fear kneeling helpless in front of the brittle reflection of the power of creation

I am the particle that had the privilege of knowing you

The hand free brush, in the air floating, awaiting the artist's muse, the pose

The frail butterfly landing on the rose

Who am I?

"That which does not enter my brain shall not have reason to enter my heart, and if it does through misguided goodness or weakness, it shall not dwell, but leave like an unwanted guest to whence it came from, for reason is the only guardian to the sanctity of my brain." - *Thus, shall be written as an introduction to myself.*

A Lapse

I touched the sunrise with my eyes
Unfurled the truth from the depth of my lies

The clouds lit burning bright

The bay, brushing its confines, revealed an endless ocean

My steps silent, my body stagnant, but my soul in motion

I remembered how it all began

In my mental records I saw your wisdom

I knew what was and is to be

The disk golden, a glimpse of your temper

Giving life without sum, generosity looking at the futile selfish counting machine of man

Beauty and innocence facing the ugly battalion's drum

The uncontrolled progression of life laughing at the pretence of the steady captain at the helm

The waves slowly breathed, the earth receded

Silent particles made a stream

The ocean uttered an unrecognizable silent scream

The wind bid farewell to the air
The breeze vanished, split between vapour made fair

The liquid carpet unfurled

As the world it's balance perceived
The soft voice of a recurring time heaved

Beyond the darkness and abyss
Presumptions and greed

Human walls made of gold and steel
Sheer helplessness and fears

Pouring yet forgiving tears
Because and why bent in front of the power to heal

The sun floating in mid air
The orb promising a treat and a dare

Should the vision be blurred?
Should the hearing be endured?

The rays of hope be but felt?

Should the purpose of today be questioned?

Experience the life that is

See the light that be

On Legacy

There are amongst the dead those who leave behind a vicious odour due to their nefarious deeds during their lifetime. I hope that the memory of me will be as agreeable as those of the embalming of gratitude and richer in recollections of goodness than the brightest colours of tulips.

On Self-Definition

Think thyself yourself.

Her

She makes the words speak
She makes the dreams dream

To find her is to suffer a wreckage and land in paradise

To speak to her is to hear her eyes, tears in mine, my anchor in disarray

Written is my story along with hers, I resume as a shadow among the clouds

I think I will find her again one day

Yet, it is a forever I await, I and her, I contemplate

The rose is my destiny, my itinerary of tomorrow

There, I find her extended hand, a tender look

I search for her without a compass, but her shadow accompanies the mirror of my will

The eyes saddened, the heavens advise me to wait, "You will find her at the rendezvous; to be one you need to be two."

Full of regrets, I do know myself lost without her

I want her

Of her I can

The truth from the lie,

She is everything

An irredeemably irrefutable proof

I seek her in my memories

I believe her to be anchored in my image

Beyond the doubt, certainty

You, my guide, my star

My rose

On Work Colleagues

We all know of each other, but hardly each other.

Testing Humankind

Religions, being capitalistic in nature, encouraged the idea of reward for efforts, and extended the concept to the

Divine, yet it does not seem to perceive that life is free, the sun never asks for a commission or reward in exchange for its rays, and that the ideas of sin, punishment, and reward for good deeds, while inherent to the functioning of human societies, have no place in nature.

Therefrom I conclude that the idea of a Maker testing us has equally no place; for nature is beyond good and evil.

Playing to the vanity of humankind, religion propagated the idea of us figuring it out. How Clever we are! Let us measures the vibrations of our selves in infinity.

On Being Lost

A piece of wood lost in the ocean seeking a destiny.

On Learning from mistakes

"I feel stupid, I should not have made that mistake." Said an apprentice.

"It is ok. Looking stupid will make you remember your errors, so that you can learn. Just try not to make the same mistakes multiple times as that would mean a lack in character and not a lapse in judgement." Said his instructor.

On Conscience

Is the consciousness of a human being alien to nature? Is it possible that nature has a similar conscience? A conscience that moves unawares of itself, as propitious, invariably individual and elusive. Is it possible that this conscience is humanity?

On Books

You can't have a conversation with your descendants when you are dead, but they can when they are alive; write a book!

You

I do remember the cries of birds

The sound of the ships speaking to the oars

I see sirens inviting sailors to a sea in delirium

A peril seeking a haven even a shipwreck

I see her face of the softness of a rose

A glimpse towards a dream that believes itself to be real

A heart which beats in order to find its soul

The mountains lost in the depths of their entrails

Lovers kissing each other under the severe watchful eyes of the sentry

I see you; my wish against the fate of the ticking clock

I imagined you so not to lose you

I find you in the beauty of the bay, the colour of the sea, the benevolence of the sun,

The largesse of your fine body

The indigo of your eyes

The sustained will of your heart

My trajectory towards you flows

The heart that beats so not to expire

The waves of the future remind me of my past

I find you off the coast of my heart, a sigh, a journey, an "I love you"

A promise of our days to come, I see

The benevolent gaze of good fortune into itself

The underpinning of the future is a good return

The art of loving, a will of two, a conscience to be moved

Facing the odds together in an embracing excess

On Maturity

"You bring people down so that you can rise up, you obviously do not know how to soar." – *To the people who point their fingers to others so to hide their deficiencies*

Contradictions

Time with no clocks or clicks

Youth with strength and beauty await

What is it all worth?

Fortune with no Grace, charm or common sense

Zebras confused calling themselves mustangs

Hyenas smiling like dogs
Sharks showing their teeth trying to come across as dolphins

Politicians hanging around an honest woman

A genuine and descent smile where is it to be found?

Freedom to soar, to dive deep, and fly

To be and continue to be

In the darkness to shine and glow

To give hope and sustenance

Like the sun to be generous, yet be untouched by mediocre minds

To shine with endless light

To find the wisdom of life and hang around for a longer time

How does it all work and was it ever meant to be?

On Heaven, Hell and Computers

They say that before you die, life flashes before you, I like to think that it is a final shutdown where your brain reassesses all the processes of your life, you relive the most significant part of it for the last time; hell is but all the shit you handed to others coming to you at once seeking revenge. Heaven, the good deeds parading in front of you, saluting you and saying, "Your life was worthwhile."

On Valuable People

"As impactful as the sun when it comes as when it leaves." - *On the value of those exceptional people we were privileged to meet and now have to say goodbye to*

Signs of Madness

"They are all paranoid." Apparently, this voice does not see itself in the "all" of dementia.

On What we are

Is it possible that we are more than what we are?

The Polyglot

If I were a magician or a poet,

I would say pure is "echte"
I would say fire is hot, but "fuego" is best
I would call water "aqua" and "air" air
I would call passion a link to her
But I am neither, so I just look puzzled and dumb

In evidence some invisible things you can't just live without

If every river intends to find its sea

Every mountain rising to greet the dawn and every offing dreaming to become a horizon

My thoughts randomly to her call
My heart to her missing presence beat their clicks

Every laughter is a "lachaln" in disguise every smile a "rizada" awaiting its time

If I were a sculptor, I would give up sculpting and a painter I will become for in painting I may find my muse in the colours inspired by her eyes

Egotism Made Apparent

When you are drunk with yourself you don't hear your loud voice, yet everyone else does. Your obnoxiousness is evident to all but you.

On Boredom

Boring rises everyday, boring gives life to the world. If interesting is intrepid, boring is safe for it is solar.

On Knowing What You Want

If you don't know what you want avoid what you don't want, that in itself is a good start.

A Short Bio

I was born on a planet named after a rock

Humble was my beginning, I was born without first being

Unable to talk, crying was the first significant thing I did before I learned to walk

Like a parrot I repeated everything thing I heard

And through no fault of mine, it was assumed that I learned to talk

Later on, without being instructed, I observed and measured

They thought me a cute colt from the way on four I tried to reach a table, a counter,

I stood up and of the world I begged to differ

My reach was not to beg or curve my straight spine in humiliation

I learned to learn from my hard-learned lessons

To see the world through my own eyes and ask for forgiveness lest I become an igneous piece of matter

I learned to make room where there was none, beyond my ego and delusions

Laugh at laughter and perceive the illusion of survival

Through the thickness of my sorrow I stumbled upon the wisdom of the usefulness of a broken arrow; its end always points to a direction

On Your Place in the World

"Do you do this to annoy me?" Asked a person of the universe

"Perhaps not everything that is done is about you." Responded the universe.

On Sense, Order and Beauty

If life doesn't make sense, how come it has an order? If it has an order how come it does not make sense? Sense and order are the two distinct features of our lives; are they opposites of each other or do they compliment each other? If they do; are we orderly senseless products of life? Are we sensible disordered beings?

Is orderly senseless orderly?
Is senseless order orderly?
Is orderly senseless sensible?

Is senseless order sensible?
Is a disorder sensible?

Let us rephrase the above by adding a minor detail:

Is an orderly senseless person orderly?
Is a senseless orderly person orderly?
Is an orderly senseless person sensible?
Is a senseless orderly person sensible?
Is a disordered person sensible?

What is the point of ugliness and beauty in all of this?

On Life

Life is not the problem, life is a solution. Those who think it to be endured are miserable souls and their views were shaped by negative energy, those who believe that there is anything better, are misled by their urge to live eternally and are apparent witnesses to the greatness of life since they want more of it and not less.

I know that life under a human form is a gift, few creatures get the privilege to experience it as such; to whatever cause I had the chance to experience it in its fullness in a positive way, I am utterly grateful.

The Eagle

An eagle, in the morning, to the expanse of the heaven his gaze he sends

He sees his future with a thud

He sheds a tear, it falls from his nest to the world below, which sees it as a sign; the beginning of a fall

The drop crashes on a flower for a while now thirsty of life,

It reciprocates through an increase of its desire to bloom despite the strife,

It seems to perceive the primary reason for its existence;

The flower secretes a fluid which takes the form of a dew

The dew is overpowered by the wind which reduces it to vapour as bright as the sun

Cruel destiny of an eternity on the run

Bees, all trapped by the banners of a spider, seek a salutary exit under the desperate gaze of the predator; do they sense their end palpable?

The vapour shatters against the banners of the monster now in complete inertia,

Splinters the wind the waiting lines of dementia

Free, the bees find a refuge and a sense

Their miniscule steps cling to the dust of gratitude,

It carries the order of balance; every being to itself must find a seed in its solitude

The powder spreads wherever their tracks mingle with the febrile look of flowers;

They wake up from their deathly life with a colour in their hearts

The horror faces the fatal beautiful aurora

Birth vanquishes death

Every seed is a rebirth

Is metamorphoses a wish for an absence?

Change a new cadence?

Bloom the flowers with the colours of tomorrow, yet there is no visible hand

No footsteps left on the tracing sand

What does the fate of a heart and the sound of the avalanche hide?

What does a tomorrow want except a trend!

Religion as a Soporific Agent

"Religions can be a lullaby, but you have to be willing and ready to sleep in order for them to have an effect on you."
- *On individual responsibility and the myth that religion is the source of all superstitions.*

On the End

Through the thickness of the veil of time and missed opportunities

The wires of the souls married in the absentia of the mind

The realization that it is you that the heart awaits beyond its blurred vision

Beyond the doubts and recriminations of itself
Every dissected and reshaped thought of you

The strings of imagination playing tunes unknown

The mastery of the disposition of time, its mood untidy

The sun on the bay

The vibrations of the past through a subtle inclination in the present intertwined

The echoes of time in the hollow clocks of humankind

The perception in the perceived thought

The object and the self rising in endless tides

The flowers withstanding the cruel winter, coming back in the summer in waves of beautiful petals and perfumed intentions

To the death of me I speak with a smile for I saw your shallow mind

Beaten every time by the birth of a child, you hover like an insect,

I perceive you as lonely as time, and you are but the sum of your despair in the face of a conquering life

The moon watching the night, a speck of darkness in a world of light

Because of the day being mostly longer than the night

The summer forgiving the treacherous fall

Hope lighter and wiser than despair

I see it also in the brightness; gathered pearls in empty space defying the abyss; from Earth I am looking straight down to the void of the world some call the night

It is winter, you don't scare me, I lived long enough to be imbued by the summer breeze

I am not in defiance for your end is equally mine,

To observe is the power of my kind

The world aware of itself

We pass on not to fade, but to linger in perception

We seek not to find

We are measure of the stars, in envy they look through the night

Humans in love's ecstasy intertwined

On Omnipotence

"If God can make anything, can God make a "square-circle?" Asked a mathematician.

"Let me check my book." Responded a man of the book.

On the Mean Spirited

"He has the venom on in his mouth; he must discharge it." - *On the brutal persons who are always seeking new victims*

On Religion, Morals, and Teaching

Apparently, according to religion, God lacks basic pedagogical skills since his teaching methods involve, among others things, many warnings, and if his pupils don't get his sense of order, he passes on, not necessarily in the same order, to earthquakes, floods, pestilence, plagues, diseases, mayhem, jihad, corporal punishment, inquisition, burning of people at the stakes, witch hunts, and always with no fail, favours iniquities and racism against women.

This is certainly a hell of a classroom.

The Matter

They call me, well, they have no name for me, swelling and swirling with delight, I know no darkness my way is the light

The one becoming one

Through space tempered with time, I am heading for another spark

I see her in the night, she is the way, my purpose the only one I see in sight
Andromeda, her name I call in the dark

The longer I wait, the greater is the urge,
Existence, the range of my being
No insignificance of black holes is bound to impede my wingless flight

I see her dance as I surge
To her I am bound
We are two in billions of billions, but ourselves we found

Through existence you may not hear us, but you may see the sound of our approach

You may mistake our motion for an illusion

If you pay attention, you can surpass the confusion

The two becoming one
Two world merging

The one becoming one

I measure not through your clicks and clocks

I do not move on liquid or rocks

Air is too heavy to carry my weight

Fear, hate and segregation, I leave them to locks

To humanity, I leave a testament with light

To live is to die

To die is not to pause, but to be re-composed

It is the story of matter; an endless transformation

It is a galactic wisdom and a human observation

Life asks, "Don't you hear me as I vanquish nothingness through matter?"

"Just watch me!" Says a voice, "Parts of me rearranged, I am living further. "

Hear me I'm the galactic matter

See me in the matter

The one becoming many

You may mistake our motion for an illusion
If you pay attention, you can surpass the confusion

I see her in the night, she is the way, my purpose the only one I see in sight

Andromeda, her name I call in the dark

A small dot becoming a point, becoming a word, becoming a world, a matter of perception

I don't remember what or when I started my projection

Certain I am of my destination

I am the horizon in motion

On Control

Many times, in life, you have opportunities and options, but not control. And when you are lucky the illusion of control is given to you; this is when you make symphonies.

On Feeling Down

Whenever you feel down, remember it is always daylight somewhere on this rock we call Earth. Whenever you are belittled by a human, remember that she or he does not represent the whole for the earth is way bigger than any puny creature you may encounter.

On God and the Afterlife

Through religion humans worship all the contradictory qualities of life yet deny it through the substitution of it by the words "God" and a promise of an "Afterlife".

On the Proud and the Shy

The first has the pride of the abyss and second the timidity of the tomb.

On the Invisible God

Since God, if there's one, has decided to be invisible and impalpable to the rest of us, I decided to live my life the same way; I am quite content, no hard feelings here, not to have him or her in my life.

If God has his or her reason to be in hiding, then who am I to attempt to bring about a visible semblance of him or her in my world. Wouldn't that be a blasphemy? And isn't that exactly what all religions do?

On Population Control

We need laws, but not control. We need babysitters, but not babying, we also need police, but no policing.

Some of us believe that they should be herded; that is their choice. This being said, the rest of us will pass for we are autonomous beings who need no shepherding or big brothers.

To the Muse

I am harvesting the words of the muse

She is love incarnate

True companion in the days of friendship's drought

The voice of reason intertwined with passion innate

My fate as I write it in pulses as light as air and solid as steel

My life unfurling its bits, told through footprints in the aether,

Misconstrued words, measures of a crude, yet benevolent intent

The echoes of humanity challenging the criminal passive silence of the gods

The daring dance of the infant to the invisible rhythm of the willing universe

Logic, a weapon against the gnawing force of rust and the sheer brutality of rods

The word becoming a verse

Through the clouds, the daybreak trying to be born

Diamonds in darkness awaiting the rays of prospect;
The heart willingly sailing the sea of passion at the risk of being torn,

The miner with a weary hand to feed a loved child,

The groom to the bride, to demonstrate his love, confused with tribal respect

True love boring past anger, disrespect, ice and fire, extending a bruised hand that is to its companion meek as mild

The summits of the Andes at sunrise anticipating the condor

The depth of the ocean asking what are pigments and colour in its darkness for?

To the hasty judgement, a lump of solidified rocks recklessly flying into space; just another tomb

To the discerning eye, a living matter; a floating womb

To my kind our lovely home

Each person a constellation

Every renewed desire an object
moving to a target; life in motion; a
significant sign of being alive

Life from the shadows painting itself
at each dive

No destination, no plans to arrive

The muse of itself aware

The truth of the lie made bare

The question asking the answer to
dare

Our Individual History

Luckily for us, our story is lived by us
and told to us by no other creatures but
ourselves. Otherwise our anodyne

existence will be so shocking to us that we may take the risk of not wanting to relive it again.

A Prayer to the Deep

Passing, the imminence of the unavoidable end

That which was a mere dare at youth is for older age an exorbitant fare

Life finally understood at the edge of the carnivorous abyss

The will to go on, yet the predatory life consumes itself; a mesh to the candle in activity to death bound

No anger, but a conclusion found

Like billions before me, taking stock of the final time in reluctance we space

Staring at what is to be not to be

The distance in projection to face

The urge to live dumbfounded by the unexpected pace

Of the stars I borrow a parting art

With grace to return to the start

Of hell I accuse no reception, but that which our kind can make

The birth of a star in fission; Earth unrecognizable

Staring at the floating helm, the rest of my ship in tatters

The floodgates of the ocean, hurricanes unbound

The night creeping on the sailing moon

Watching and hoping for Poseidon to hear its desperate tune

On Life and Death

Life is extraordinary, death is not, it is a cessation of life and as such ordinary; empty space is full of it.

A momentum

Find a sun, a pearl, a shoreline

Seek a star, a galaxy, a wreck

Another you, a gaze that looks at you with the largesse of the horizon

A sea with a landmark
A shadow amongst the clouds
A subterranean brilliance

Run like runs the watercourse

With the precision of a swallow swimming in the air

Look at me as you look at yourself in the mirrors

A pearl amongst the stars

Set course for a destiny as difficult as that of honesty

As clear as goodness

A love as recurrent as are the waves on vacation

The beaches awaiting the returning promises

Another you that make you better

Who finds you thirsty of her presence

A shelter beyond the infamous waves

A fission that becomes one

As sweet as the product of the bees

As truthful as an awakening and as lucid as alertness

Fly beyond the debility of borders,
nations, religions and bad dreams

Surpass the nightmares of those who
divide to better impoverish

Learn from the sage by seeing his
humble abode
A tomorrow with no obstruction
codes

Be better than a wreck
Master your disarray as is done by
the swallow
The lovers of tomorrow
The wind and horizon

Be inspired by the moon, a single
solitude amongst the stars

Listen to the music of dolphins
The laughter of children

Being in perpetual exchange
Growth towards the deep heights
The common of muscles and valves

Life; a rest on the run

Above all find sustenance, nourish yourself from the horizon
Take probing puffs, dance like the children do
Give with no reason except for the appreciation of goodness as a gift

Emerge from the shadows like do the waves
Be subtle as the rainbow

Become a sun during the threatening winter
Be brave under tyranny like the one who stood alone on a square facing a moving tank

Free and richer by seeing such a being in effervescence

Become human like the sun wants you to be
A moon, stars
An earthly brilliance

Beyond your body that is forsaking
you
Of your soul in drought
Of your coiling in December
The June of your passing

Run beyond your own being

Rise up out of your time, do you see
yourself floating?

A being dying but awake

The paradox of the universe is you
Improbable but yet
Being in the era of time

Insatiability for life, the reason of
your birth

Desire, the cause of your
Benevolence

To continue, the verb of your
movements

Maturity, the goal of your intent

Spread your wings, race towards the horizon

Succumb to the extent of the seasons

Find a sun, a pearl, a shoreline

Seek a star, a galaxy, a wreck

A Divine Predicament

It does truck me as odd that the thing that supposedly created all this, does not seem willing to self manifest or partake in the struggle to make its existence apparent, while all of us spend time trying to debate its existence, some of us killing each other for it, while the simple solution would be for it to just physically appear to us like we do to each other and end the debate once for all.

This is evidently either not important to it or it does not exist; in either cases we are left alone in a predatory world trying to kill us and which will most certainly succeed.

When in Love

I do not see my passing as an end or a beginning

A wave is always followed by a wave

I am sure you can relate

The obliterated sun will rise in time, shadows may traverse the horizon, but constant is its line

In insignificance we will shake hands
In memory we will also merge

I would have liked to meet you one more time and say,

You are more precious than rain under the torching sun

More vivid than gratitude in an ocean of selfishness

More palpable than desire and despair

When the object is there and the odds are against

You seem not to know that you are precious

The right mirror is mired away from your eyes

I can see the reflection

You give colour to the sea

You give measures to the mountains

Your name they whisper when they extend their summits surreptitiously looking behind the clouds

Closer are the heavens when you are

Colourless they all are when you are not around

I never know what you are thinking, but of your presence are the drops of rain or are those tears in my eyes?

The muse says you are trouble, she is working overtime
I think it is all misconception for you look alike

I can traverse the horizon and I see no line
Except, your figure and the look you gave me when we parted ways

The ghosts of potential are mired
They claim they have been misled
They were promised achievement, they say, instead they are staring at a feeble line

Up upon the shoulders of the mountains, I think I can see your face

Reason says it is an illusion

I am inclining further, it is you the stars are reflecting

I measure the distance, I am right, it is you that yonder sun beaming

The ice my resolve attempts to shatter
I feel no freezing rays, instead melting is the winter in its last attempts

Summer in me is rising

Tulips the northern ice God shrouding

I feel your presence

Can you relate?

The Quasar and the Star

A quasar asked a star, "what I am to you?"

She replied, "whenever you leave, my constellation is the Big Dipper
My soul leaves traces behind, like milky spots my tears give away their traits
You are the good thing that awaits

The spark in the light
The light in me in the night

The link in the chain
Humility, antidote to the vain

If you don't come back there is no evidence of me ever being bright

You make me want to rise like the one sun

You make feel for the many yet lonely vibrations of the drums"

Looking forlorn, the quasar his mind in particles
His heart, brighter than ten suns, shines, and says,

To you my projected arrow aims

Every time I part, a piece of me I leave

You are at the heart of the matter

My thoughts in the darkness, you they seek

Drifting in the abyss of a world without you

I know how it feels to rise with a light, but be bleak

If I don't come back to you, I will have for a heart a black hole

Of me a life and the destiny of inanimate coal

Of life, I feel I may be forced, like the clouds covered sun grieving for the day, to take a leave

I see Andromeda heading to the Milky Way, an encounter I observe

Sure, the dust will clear

The clouds will disappear

What is true today should be true the next day

Just like pain is engulfed in sorrow

If you can't see the road find a way

Doesn't that sun yonder shine today as it did yesterday, as it will do tomorrow?

Transfused by what they heard, the stars were awakened, and in the darkness opened their sails looking like billions of open eyes

The universe vibrated

On Earth, the deep silent lagoons in the eternal night for the first time saw light

Life teamed, elevating electric thunder copulating with liquid, giving in ecstasy birth to what might

Potential even in the darkness

Lightness in the light

On the Pursuit of Knowledge Vs. Gold

"The pursuit of knowledge is better than the pursuit of gold." Said the East India Company, through its Haileybury College Medals, to its students, and then it sent them away in pursuit of gold.

On Self-Fulfilling Prophecies

Sometimes, you may encounter the very negative situations you tried to avoid, and if you do, be alert to the fact that you did your best to avoid them, lest some misconstrued regrets, tending to poison your prospects, attempts to convince you that all your efforts were in vain.

Remember that you at least tried to avoid evil and were no slave to chance.

The Usefulness of Gratitude

Gratitude in dire environments is good because it finds a reserve of positivity where there is none visible to the fatigued eyes and the tirelessly prospecting mind.

Love Wrapped in The Present

Love may sometimes be a gift, but you have to earn it to keep it.

On Changing the World

You can wait a hundred years for the world to change to your liking or you can improve yourself, which is much easier to do as you have control over the whole process; you can do this now, this right moment and be better equipped to handle it.

Just an Observation

You may unfurl the stratosphere in search of a heavenly father

You may dream of bronze, gold, diamond, toil for treasures

You may concede your time and space as allotments for future gains

You may measure your distance by the speed of your progression

You may think your soul of the nature of feathers;
Lightness in the stature of your delusions

You may find safety in the insignificance of imbalance

You may pledge to strike a deal with life in the form of premeditation

You may ask for forgiveness, but forget to commit your words to deliverance

Know that the future awaits no matter how much you anticipate

The only thing divine is what lies in your perception

The only treasures worth giving are those you are not willing to share

The only lasting commodity to gather is the present

The only advancement is the one measured by the speed of creative thought

Know that the arrangements of reason follow stricter patterns

Life has no creed, blind it is to temptation, the only temperature it measures is that of its unpredictable disposition
It is not bound to dealings and forgives no moving creation

The only display it cares about is in the wisdom of your interpretation

The price of soundness is responsible measures

The only forgiveness is the one you are willing to give

You may want to listen while you still can

You may want to perceive while you still see

You may want to love while you still have a heart that beats

It knows the gift of being powered by ordered validations

You may want to check the picture of your essence in the reflections of your deeds

Find the recurring lines of your habitual diversions to lead you to the source of your sadness

Find the purpose of your despair
Gauge the colours of your shallow shadows
The unmistakable surge of your pretenses

Your spaceship may lead you to places, but not before your thoughts fly you there

Your accumulations are as much a burden as a shudder

Your dreams of the one to find may well be the one of another in possession

You may be asked whether to steel or walk away with the lightness of feathers

The ghosts of your decisions may be resuscitated by evident circumstances in another time, another place

Under the deafening light you may not understand the ramifications, though you are startled by the trace,
In the invisibility of the stratosphere you recognize the face

All things that matter tend to be lost

Chaos is sometimes the tool used to tame and mold your desperation

It is for someone an income

The fading attention you give yourself is the measure of success of the hidden vultures

A good way to know yourself is to ask how much of it is yours
How much of it was part of elapsed generations?
How much is but a reflection with no hint of previous detection?
The echoes of another world, of other beings

Are you the simile of a headline or a deeper understanding?

Know that the horizon is an opportunity
Walls are not just meant to hide prisoners, but also to exterminate perspectives

Revolutions are doomed attempts to justify the evidence of already altered situations

Like the premonition of what is already here

They serve the purpose of illusion

Change does not come sudden it is a realization of a long progression
To the dormant only, mosquitoes' vibrations cause a shudder

Know that as true as is your existence to living, it is not equal, but the last is another sphere

Those in cowardly disguise are still hiding in defiance

In mortal expectation, we also meet our unburdened selves

In turbulence we meet the company
of fear rising to greet the surface

In the benevolence of today we meet
tomorrow's community of joy

In the words we do not say out of
respect we also give ourselves a chance;

Linear is our precarious position in
space

In mental surrender, hijacked is our
conscience

In time indefinite I meet you in the
same space though not the same time

In ports of positions I speak to your
soul

My experience to you is extended

Broken glass sounding the end of our
crass

Shadows of entitlement; despots on our goodwill

Traders of vain titles, schooled in desperation

The futility of attached intellect to a class

The voice of vanity calling the pompousness of the shrill

How and who would fit the bill?

Subtle is the pass

Fast is the motion

On comparison

It makes you look at what don't have and forget what you have.

Small Steps

"It is little keys that open up big doors." - *On small steps leading to great achievements*

On Love

If and when infatuation passes on and you still have infatuation for the same person then you may have love.

Choices

Some think that cases of treasure may shine brighter than the self-radiating sun

That the warmth of soft cushions of palaces may surpass the surface of a soft hand of a loved one

Some think that courage is being part of a winning band
And not being the last one fighting a losing battle trying to tame the moving sand

Some court the glow of diamonds and gold
Chasing the bought and that which later will be sold

If you choose, better choose that which moves
The living, the human in humanity that is alive

Currency is as current as is water to fire

There are no demons except the ones we make

There are no more alive than those living

On Positive and Negative Thoughts

Negativity is but a distraction. Positivity was, is, and must always be you; a positive number and an addition to this world when you were born.

Being

Off the clocks and clicks of your world I rise

The stars on my surge I leave behind

Light years ahead projected in time

If in pain, know that you still feel

If in joy, know that you are sheathed

The living is the envy of the dead

My eyes to the Quasars fly

Brighter than suns and galaxies my voyage surpasses

Across the ages I impart

My flight supersedes the clarity of the aether

My story told by the nebulae as they are revealed by the inquisitive eyes

Though long gone I depart

Buried in the myth is a presence

Faster than the speed of light is the speed of imagination bathing in illumination

Never out of nature even when you are not,

You carry on

Your destination will find you

A mark in existence reshuffled by the might of time

An echo in the sound

An atom in fission you were, another atom in fission you will become

Energy awaits

No resurrection but an awaiting transformation for certain

A time to go home

To become a thousand thoughts

Like the sun fade away

To be when you are not

What of you might become

A propulsion

On Relationships

Those who consider people bridges will use them.

Those who view people as humans will try to befriend them.

Those who see their partners as persons they can dump are bound to attract dumpsters and doomed they are to attract but the trash bins.

On the Balance

The sky the colours of hell

The waves splitting the heart of rocks

The wind, an angry invisible force unleashed

The trees shaken like leaves in the autumn's atomic burst

The earth barely holding to its orbit

The sun worn out, yet piercing through the thick veil of the clouds regardless

An icy temper slowly wrapped the living with an urge

To survive one must abide by the unpredictable rules of life

Like a creature of the deep he emerged from the unseen

Angrier than Belfast on a trenched Sunday

I saw him walk like Hannibal through the tamed Alps, startled I was until he said, "She loves, and I love her too."

His smile cleared the sky

His eyes calmed the seas as the wind was apparently made a relaxing breeze

Valleys of the deep gave lights
The sun burst and the summer breathed; he laughed,

His face was reflected in a mirror of an opening glass door

The joyful stranger in love was I, as I was, as I wanted to be

I heard the wind near me blow
He faded away like a spirit of light

The sea eating the rocks
The sky a colour of hell

The wind, the truth trying to bend

Unlike him, unfortunate, my present a hostage of a humanity drowning in the sand

Into the future I started to roam

I was a vanquished Hannibal looking at Rome

More cautious than Tel Aviv, yet equally desperate looking for a friend

Yet, of his knowledge as a potential, I was richer than Nathan in his best dreams

Cleverer than Satan in his deceit

Calmer than Poseidon among the tormenting seas

A voice in me said, "Balance is not an equation but a sense."

I saw the separation wall of presumptions fade away

Its concrete and steel ashamed of
their purpose

I remembered a tale of a caged Merlin
The fading lines of a divide in Berlin

I perceived humanity's children
playing on both sides of the trench

Like flowers blooming on the hardest
surfaces of rocks

The wall desperate of such an
existence started to break

The dust of time making its last blow

Its tears in bits of rocks falling like
leaves in time

I learned that there will be peace as
sure as there is the end of me

As sure as there is water in a sea

You would rejoice if you could also
into the future see

On Our Destiny

Humanity can never achieve
perfection, but it can be beautiful, herein
lies our consolation.

One Thing Deities Never Got to
The Bottom Of

In the beginning, as God made the
world he set the plants to consume rays
of the sun, a great idea in the beginning,
but then, infallibly changing his mind
halfway through, he made them
carnivorous. He then, through a
predatorial design, made animals eat
plants and each other, they in turn to be
devoured by humankind, and
invariably through the seas and

earthquakes all to be entombed and engulfed alive.

He turned to our kind and said, "Better be just for I am the judge."

As we can observe, justice and fairness are not part of nature, luckily for us we were dumb enough to accidentally invent them and brave enough, when we saw their intrinsic value, to cherish and fight for them. This, I dare say, is what make us better than all of the gods we imagined.

On Decency

It is hard to fake decency. I observed.

What We Know

We know least of ourselves

Less of the others
More or less of each other

Time is our only master
Age not our enemy, but a friend of
whom we have to let go
Kinda like you

Wisdom, we have to find
Some time we are lucky enough, it is
staring at us like the sun
Kinda like you do when you look at
me

Prosperity is a progress beyond
riches
Power is a dumb idea everyone has
and no one possesses
We have it when we learn to let go
Kinda like when you say, "Hello"

Beauty, it is in the wings of the
butterfly landing on a rose

The ease of flight of the falcon floating on air as it rises beyond our efficient yet crude attempts of imitation

It is like you when I first you saw you;
Elegance, nobility with no arrogance

The one thing truly wanted and seen through a fence

The things we say only to ourselves are the things hard to swallow and the least said
Like every time when I see you leave and I do not know how to say bye

Fame, an illusion, a pact with the arbitrary
Something the cautious try to live without; a salary

Fire is it not just something that light, it is also something that burns
Kinda like the urge to see you when you are not and are around

Missing you like empty dark spaces
miss the light

Your waters to quench my thirst
Your company to make sense of my
mind

Loneliness is a walk I am used to take
before we met
Now its seeks your semblance in
advance; to see you is its only bet

The high tides and waves are a
pleasant surf if you are prepared

Love is a quicksand better have agile
hands
Treading is not the answer

You don't hide from cancer

Need to get the antidote, the truth
from mediocrity

Lift the veil of indecency

Live for only life there is

Beyond death seeking you

Try not, but attempt

In rebirth you will find the light

Kinda like when I found you

Who would have thought?
That which is missing is that which
you been staring at all this time

Reflections have a single pursuit; to
be detected

May days are the infants of April; in
your urgency remember the source and
your intent

All that which leads is bound to
follow

A commitment unbound is as good as its people without which it is just graffiti on a wall

Love's vibrations we may not see until it is the only presence

Kinda like you when in me your gravity you settled

Ghosts of the living inhabiting the yet undead

Torments of all that could be

The blind in this can also see

The seemingly dead sea perjured through its depths
Life unfurling through what breeds underneath

Hope in "to become" despair is in not being

Mental stagnation is a sure progress
to one's prospects starvation

An agile mind carries less weight
around,

Substance is the matter of elevation

Kinda like you

On Being Dead

A perspective of when you are dead,
as you can observe beyond fear and
grief, is that you become not one thing,
but many; an endless potential of
possibilities; a tomorrow.

On Learning from Other's
Experiences

We may not always have the same
experiences, but life tends to draw

parallels for those who want to see, an education for them it will be, though the intentionally blind may not see.

The People

The people are the known unknown variable.

Love at First Sight

If it exists, better pray that love at first sight happens on the opportune time, for what guarantees do you have that the love of your life or you would not be subjects to its spell and gravity for other people at a later point in time?

This mechanism that seems to be a great blessing to you now way well turn into a curse later.

On Living by The Rules of Others

Did you ask permission to come to life? So why are you asking permission now to live other than on your own terms?

Corruption as a Challenge

Let every attempt of corrupting you be an unwelcome opportunity to be honest. Don't waste it.

On What I Know

I know more of nothing than of anything

The wise is a fool aware of the reasons for his sorrow

His mind on the opportune moment recovering a key memory

The fool is the one who thinks wisdom to be an incessant state of mind

Equilibrium

I rise from the depth of darkness my only light is who I am

I may burn my way away at night

You may think me vain cause I shine

Yet, my rays vanquish the barricades
The wall of hate, the mountains in displeasure bursting out angry through the heart of the earth

I give life and take none, at least it never is my intent

You may think me weak as I concede to the stars a measure of space

As I die at the end of the day, it is but a state in which I rise

Behold my soul on the colours of the horizon

My power in the grace of a child
My will unbound as my rays it finds

My reflections are mine and power from others I borrow none

My memories are in your heart, if I fade please soldier on

Through the depth of darkness, I cast
essence; a reflection on the moon

I may fade, but here I am

Remember me for I am you; a spark
in an endless ocean of light

I meet you in lines cast in particles
sweeping the weight of time

My words are my link to your mind

Grasp what you need on your way to
find balance

Be not ashamed as is not the Earth of
its scars,
Rivers, canyons forging through the
daybreak and night

Be humble like the curves of currents
Be brave like the one who cares not
what comes next
Yet careful not to maim a child

Be a leader of no men, but one who inspires all

Live on the Earth not engulfed in a tomb, a prisoner of palaces and slums

Kick away the dust trying to keep you down

Like me, you were born to rise

In death you will meet those you call family and friends

Mistake me not for I am not the infant of chance

I know no fate for what I do is freedom innate

I seek no worship, trade no favours for thanks

I made you tall not to crawl

I made you strong so you can lift yourself and others when you care

I made you think so you find your
way not mine

Even if you forget, I remember to
wake you up
Yet you believe you are alone

Our way is the same no matter where
you birth from

Our paths see each other in parallel

Here I am

I rise from the depth of darkness my
only light is who I am

Make me proud as I fade and shine

ABOUT THE AUTHOR

Lamine Pearlheart is an avid reader and, as far as he remembers, he always had a great appreciation for literature, history, philosophy, poetry, and enjoys long walks as a meditation form.

One of his chief interests is the understanding of the human experience in its multidimensional aspects as is apparent in his books.

He also has a passion for languages; he speaks English, French, German, Spanish and Portuguese.

The author is currently working on his first novel.